Penguin Education

Attitudes and Behaviour

Edited by Kerry Thomas

Penguin Modern Psychology Readings

General Editor
B. M. Foss

Advisory Board
Michael Argyle
Dalbir Bindra
P. C. Dodwell
G. A. Foulds
Max Hamilton
Marie Jahoda
Harry Kay
S. G. M. Lee
W. M. O'Neil
K. H. Pribram
R. L. Reid
Roger Russell
Jane Stewart
Anne Treisman
P. E. Vernon
Peter B. Warr
George Westby

D1228954

Attitudes and Behaviour

Selected Readings

Edited by Kerry Thomas

Penguin Books

Penguin Books Ltd, Harmondsworth,
Middlesex, England
Penguin Books Inc., 7110 Ambassador Road,
Baltimore, Md 21207, U.S.A.
Penguin Books Australia Ltd,
Ringwood, Victoria, Australia

First published 1971
This selection copyright © Kerry Thomas, 1971
Introduction and notes copyright © Kerry Thomas, 1971

Made and printed in Great Britain by
Cox & Wyman Ltd,
London, Reading and Fakenham
Set in Monotype Times

This book is sold subject to the condition that
it shall not, by way of trade or otherwise, be lent,
re-sold, hired out, or otherwise circulated without
the publisher's prior consent in any form of
binding or cover other than that in which it is
published and without a similar condition
including this condition being imposed on the
subsequent purchaser

Contents

Introduction

The purpose of this book is to examine the relationship between attitudes and behaviour. The starting point for any such inquiry must be a consideration of the conceptual and operational definitions of these terms and the implications these have for any relationship between attitudes and behaviour. The sequence of Readings begins with a section on current conceptual treatments of the problem. The following sections are based on empirical studies of attitudes as predictors of overt behaviour, and the question of the relationship between attitude change and behaviour change. The final Part reassesses the logical status of the construct 'attitude' and its usefulness to social scientists, making comparisons between determinants of behaviour as studied by social psychologists and acquired behavioural dispositions used in other areas of psychology.

The study of attitudes represents a major part, and probably the historical origins, of social psychology. There is little doubt that the widespread use of the concept over the last four or five decades rests on an assumption that the study of attitudes is crucial to the understanding of social behaviour. The implicit assumption has usually been of a simple, causal relationship between a multi-dimensional conception of attitude towards a social object and specific behaviour towards that object, irrespective of situation. Allport's classical definition (1935, Reading 1) suggests this interpretation. Despite considerable evidence to the contrary much social research has continued in this vein.

Research in the social sciences is concerned not only with knowledge but with solutions to problems. The aim of a Race Relations Institute is not the academic study of hypothetical constructs such as attitudes, but rather the manipulation of changes in social behaviour between racial groups. Measurement of attitudes, studies of attitude acquisition and demonstration of attitude change following educational programmes are means to such ends. If the assumption of the existence of a fairly simple, causal relationship between attitude and behaviour is false or oversimplified, then clearly the time and money spent on research into content, development and change of social attitudes is at worst wasted, and at best a false emphasis.

The most popular conceptions of attitude are multidimensional and include affective, cognitive and behavioural components. Thus attitude represents a residue of experience, cognitive and affective, of the social object in question, *and* a response tendency towards that object. Attitude in this sense is a 'hidden mechanism' which directs behaviour. But few empirical studies of attitudes operationalize the concept in this complex way. Many papers introduce research by defining attitudes as multidimensional and then measure only one or perhaps two aspects of the concept. Frequently the empirical measures are unrelated to any theoretical position. The conclusions, however, tend to be referred to the three-component attitude construct. None of the multidimensional definitions of attitude discuss the quantitative nature of the relations between the components, so that where attempts are made to measure affect, cognition and conation there are no rules for combination of the data. It follows that even where a simple relationship between multidimensional attitude and overt behaviour is predicted it cannot be tested.

Unidimensional conceptions of attitude as total affect towards an attitude object are becoming more popular. Clearly these are, theoretically at least, easier to operationalize. But they do not necessarily make any assumptions about overt behaviour. They are essentially concerned with the input side of the process, an affective residue of experience of the object. Thurstone (1931, Reading 2) suggests that although no specific behavioural prediction can be made from knowledge of attitude as total affect, nevertheless it is likely that any overt act towards an object will be of the same affective tone as the attitude to the object. If knowledge of attitude as affect only allows behavioural predictions of this generality, then clearly social scientists must investigate other variables which act in conjunction with attitude to determine specific behaviour. Many theorists, irrespective of their conception of attitude, allow that attitudes are not the sole determinants of behaviour but that various situational factors also need to be considered. Again the general absence of specified situational factors and quantification of their effect and the nature of their interaction with attitudes preclude successful prediction of behaviour. Wicker (1969, Reading 9) discusses some of these factors.

Most theorists who treat attitudes as affect still consider that they are, amongst other factors, determinants of behaviour (Thurstone, 1931, Reading 2; Doob, 1947, Reading 4; Fishbein, 1967, Reading 5); but there is a second approach to the relationship between attitudes and behaviour which, while not precluding a causal relationship in this direction, is primarily concerned with *consistency* between attitudes and behaviour. Such consistency theorists (e.g. Insko and Schopler, 1967, Reading 3) predict that not only will behaviour tend to be consistent in affective tone with attitude but that where behaviour is suddenly or forcibly changed this will cause a change in attitude. The forced compliance studies of the cognitive dissonance school are dramatic examples of this (Festinger and Carlsmith, 1959; Linder, Cooper and Jones, 1967, Reading 13). But closer examination of these studies leads to the conclusion that although it is theoretically possible to demonstrate attitude change followed in time by behaviour change, thus implying a causal relationship, the reverse is not true. This is because overt behaviour is, by definition, observed or measured as it occurs whereas the exact time of attitude change is not revealed simply by its measurement, indeed it cannot be denoted. Therefore in the forced compliance studies although the behaviour change occurs and is measured prior to re-assessment of attitude the attitude change may have been concurrent with or even have preceded the behaviour change.

If attitude is defined as affect towards an object and behaviour towards that object is also considered in affective terms, one is in effect dealing with two attitudes: attitude towards the object and attitude towards a specific behaviour with regard to that object. Clearly there will be some overlap between these in so far as the behaviour towards the object contains phenomenological aspects of the object itself. But it seems likely that attitude towards performance of a specific behaviour will be a better predictor of the occurrence of that act than will attitude to the object of the act. In effect this is a statement that the affective residue of experience of the stimulus-in-general is likely to be less closely related to an overt act with regard to that stimulus than is the affective residue of experience of performance of the act. *Attitude to the act* incorporates the reinforcement contingencies or outcomes of performance of the act in that particular situation, and is thus more likely to take general situational variables into account. This is the approach to the prediction of behaviour used by Fishbein (1967, Reading 5).

One of the common explanations for lack of correlation between attitude and behaviour is that the stimulus object is insufficiently specific. Attitudes are often measured to a class of objects, whereas behaviour is directed at a specific example of this class (Triandis and Triandis, 1960). Apart from this, however, the phenomenological meaning of any complex stimulus is likely to be labile, to some extent, over time. Similarly, a stimulus can change its meaning across situations, e.g. 'policeman' in the context of finding a lost child, and 'policeman' in the context of riot control. It would be surprising if, for some sections of a community, behaviour towards the attitude object 'policeman' was similar in these two situations. Specificity of the response unit is also a problem. If, as DeFleur and Westie (1963, Reading 17) suggest, the correlation between attitude and behaviour is improved by severe restriction of the generality of both the attitude object and the behaviour, then the greater the improvement in prediction achieved by such means, the less general value the prediction will have for problem-oriented social scientists.

Psychologists are concerned with the study of behaviour and social psychologists are concerned with the study of social behaviour. Few people would argue in favour of a distinction between behaviour and social behaviour, yet the terminologies used for the study of these are quite different. The term attitude is rarely used outside social, personality and clinical psychology and is totally absent from general behaviourist psychology. The final section of this volume contains a selection of theoretical papers which attempt to reassess the status of 'attitude' in the context of this problem.

While it is possible that 'attitude' is an outdated concept which has survived beyond its useful life only in social psychology, it is significant that most explanatory schemes for behaviour in general psychology make use of some term which denotes or includes an affective residue of experience, whether on the stimulus side, e.g. discriminative stimulus (Skinner, 1953), or on the response side, e.g. reinforcement value (Rotter, 1954), and 'K' (Spence, 1956). Campbell (1963, Reading 21) suggests that the absence of 'attitude' from general behaviourist psychology and its presence in social psychology is in part a function of the ecology of data collection. 'Attitude' is used by most social psychologists as a 'hidden mechanism' representing a residue of experience of transaction with an object, which in turn will have some degree of influence on consequent behaviour. Social psychologists can question their subjects and obtain self-reports on the 'meaning' of the stimulus and the affect attached to it. Those psychologists who do not use the term 'attitude' often work with animals and are frequently already in possession of the organisms' relevant reinforcement history; even if they are interested in 'affective response' either to the stimulus or to the response to that stimulus, clearly a self-report is out of the question. On the other hand, direct observation of overt behaviour is relatively easy.

Finally, there is the question of emphasis. Strict behaviourists, whether animal psychologists working with rats and pigeons, or social learning theorists attempting to modify the behaviour of deviant children, are primarily interested in units of overt behaviour produced in response to variations in stimuli, and arrange direct means of observing and measuring such behaviour. The 'latent processes' are of relatively little importance. A social scientist is, however, usually in a quite different position. Here attitude measurement is intended to replace knowledge of the reinforcement history of the individual, and represents an attempt to make some assessment of probable behaviour where measurement of the behaviour itself is too complex or too costly or where the behaviour has yet to occur. Here measurement of attitude is a means to an end and interest is focused on the 'latent processes'. The emphasis cannot be on the overt behaviour, but must instead be directed towards the determinants of the behaviour. Too often this has meant measurement of attitude to over-generalized attitude objects, presented out of context. It is hoped that this collection of Readings will draw attention to the lack of success of such an over-simplified approach to the prediction of social behaviour.

References

ALLPORT, G. W. (1935), 'Attitudes', in C. Murchison (ed.), *A Handbook of Social Psychology*, Clark University Press.

CAMPBELL, D. T. (1963), 'Social attitudes and other acquired behavioral dispositions', in S. Koch (ed.), *Psychology: A Study of a Science*, vol. 6, McGraw-Hill.

DEFLEUR, M. L., and WESTIE, F. R. (1963/1964), 'Attitude as a scientific concept', *Soc. Forces*, vol. 42, pp. 17–31.

DOOB, L. W. (1947), 'The behavior of attitudes', *Psychol. Rev.*, vol. 54, pp. 135–56.

FEATHER, N. T. (1959), 'Subjective probability and decision under uncertainty', *Psychol. Rev.*, vol. 66, pp. 150–64.

FESTINGER, L., and CARLSMITH, J. M. (1959), 'Cognitive consequences of forced compliance', *J. abnorm. soc. Psychol.*, vol. 58, pp. 204–10.

FISHBEIN, M. (1967), 'Attitude and the prediction of behavior', in M. Fishbein (ed.), *Readings in Attitude Theory and Measurement*, Wiley, pp. 477–92.

INSKO, C. A., and SCHOPLER, J. (1967), 'Triadic consistency: a statement of affective–cognitive–conative consistency', *Psychol. Rev.*, vol. 74, pp. 361–76.

LINDER, D. E., COOPER, J., and JONES, E. E. (1967), 'Decision freedom as a determinant of the role of incentive magnitude in attitude change', *J. Pers. soc. Psychol.*, vol. 6, pp. 245–54.

ROTTER, J. B. (1954), *Social Learning and Clinical Psychology*, Prentice-Hall.

SKINNER, B. F. (1953), *Science and Human Behavior*, Macmillan Co.

SPENCE, K. W. (1956), *Behavior Theory and Conditioning*, Yale University Press.

THURSTONE, L. L. (1931), 'The measurement of social attitudes', *J. abnorm. soc. Psychol.*, vol. 26, pp. 249–69.

TRIANDIS, H. C., and TRIANDIS, L. M. (1960), 'Race, social class, religion and nationality as determinants of social distance', *J. abnorm. soc. Psychol.*, vol. 61, pp. 110–18.

WICKER, A. W. (1969), 'Attitudes versus actions: the relationship of verbal and overt behavioral responses to attitude objects', *J. soc. Issues*, vol. 25, pp. 41–78.

Part One **Conceptual Bases**

Any attempt to examine the nature of the relationship between attitudes and behaviour must start with a consideration of definitions. This section begins with excerpts from two influential early papers. The extract from Allport (Reading 1) contains a selection of definitions of attitude evolved prior to 1935. These are all multidimensional and almost all imply that an attitude has some directive influence on behaviour. Thurstone's definition (Reading 2) is unidimensional and contains no element of behavioural predisposition. He treats attitude simply as affect for or against an object. He does, however, state that behaviour, irrespective of its specific nature, can be expected to be of the same affective tone as the attitude. Two of the remaining papers in this section, Insko and Schopler, and Fishbein, treat attitude in the same way as Thurstone. Insko and Schopler (Reading 3) represent consistency theory. They predict that there will be a tendency, at a conscious level, to achieve consistency between attitude towards an object and the affect attached to any behaviour with regard to that object. Doob (Reading 4) uses an S–R terminology, treating attitude as a learned, mediating response essentially defined by the stimulus history of the individual; the behaviour that follows is considered as learned separately as a function of the reinforcement characteristics of the situation in which it occurs. Thus for Doob, behaviour may be unrelated to attitude. Fishbein (Reading 5) derives an equation where behavioural intention is a function, not of affect towards the object of the behaviour, but rather affect attached to the act itself. Use of attitude-to-the-act, incorporates the effects of reinforcement characteristics of performance of the behaviour. This equation also includes normative aspects of the situation in which the behaviour occurs.

1 G. W. Allport

Attitudes

Excerpts from G. W. Allport, 'Attitudes', in C. Murchison (ed.), *A Handbook of Social Psychology*, Clark University Press, 1935, pp. 798–844.

Attitudes as a form of readiness

Let us now consider a representative selection of definitions and characterizations of attitude.

[An attitude is] readiness for attention or action of a definite sort (Baldwin, 1901–1905).

Attitudes are literally mental postures, guides for conduct to which each new experience is referred before a response is made (Morgan, 1934, p. 47).

Attitude = the specific mental disposition toward an incoming (or arising) experience, whereby that experience is modified, or, a condition of readiness for a certain type of activity (Warren, 1934).

An attitude is a complex of feelings, desires, fears, convictions, prejudices or other tendencies that have given *a set or readiness to act* to a person because of varied experiences (Chave, 1928).

... a more or less permanently enduring state of readiness of mental organization which predisposes an individual to react in a characteristic way to any object or situation with which it is related (Cantril, 1934).

From the point of view of Gestalt psychology a change of attitude involves a definite physiological stress exerted upon a sensory field by processes originating in other parts of the nervous system (Köhler, 1929, p. 184).

An attitude is a tendency to act toward or against something in the environment which becomes thereby a positive or negative value (Bogardus, 1931, p. 62).

By attitude we understand a process of individual consciousness which determines real or possible activity of the individual counterpart of the social value; activity, in whatever form, is the bond between them (Thomas and Znaniecki, 1918, p. 27).

The attitude, or preparation in advance of the actual response, constitutes an important determinant of the ensuing social behavior. Such neural settings, with their accompanying consciousness, are numerous and significant in social life (F. H. Allport, 1924, p. 320).

An attitude is a mental disposition of the human individual to act for or against a definite object (Droba, 1933).

[An attitude] denotes the general set of the organism as a whole toward an object or situation which calls for adjustment (Lundberg, 1929).

[Attitudes] are modes of emotional regard for objects, and motor 'sets' or slight, tentative reactions toward them (Ewer, 1929, p. 136).

An attitude, roughly, is a residuum of experience, by which further activity is conditioned and controlled. . . . We may think of attitudes as acquired tendencies to act in specific ways toward objects (Krueger and Reckless, 1931, p. 238).

When a certain type of experience is constantly repeated, a change of set is brought about which affects many central neurons and tends to spread over other parts of the central nervous system. These changes in the general set of the central nervous system temper the process of reception. . . . In terms of the subjective mental life these general sets are called attitudes (Warren, 1922, pp. 360 ff.).

An attitude is a disposition to act which is built up by the integration of numerous specific responses of a similar type, but which exists as a general neural 'set', and when activated by a specific stimulus results in behavior that is more obviously a function of the disposition than of the activating stimulus. The important thing to note about this definition is that it considers attitudes as broad, generic (not simple and specific) determinants of behavior (G. W. Allport, 1929).

We shall regard attitudes here as verbalized or verbalizable tendencies, dispositions, adjustments toward certain acts. They relate not to the past nor even primarily to the present, but as a rule, to the future. Sometimes, of course, it is a hypothetical future. . . . The 'attitude' is primarily a way of being 'set' toward or against things (Murphy and Murphy, 1931, p. 615).

It is not difficult to trace the common thread running through these diverse definitions. In one way or another each regards the essential feature of attitude as a *preparation or readiness for response*. The attitude is incipient and preparatory rather than overt and consummatory. It is not behavior, but the precondition of behavior. It may exist in all degrees of readiness from the most latent, dormant traces of forgotten habits to the tension or motion which is actively determining a course of conduct that is under way.

A definition of attitudes

It is not easy to construct a definition sufficiently broad to cover the many kinds of attitudinal determination which psychologists today recognize, and at the same time narrow enough to exclude those types of determination which are not ordinarily referred to as attitudes. The definitions considered above contain helpful suggestions, and yet none alone is entirely satisfactory. The chief weakness of most of them seems to be their failure to distinguish between attitudes, which are often very general, and habits, which are always limited in their scope.

Any attempt at a definition exaggerates the degree of agreement which psychologists have reached, but is justified if it contributes toward securing greater agreement in the future. The following definition has the merit of including recognized types of attitudes: the *Aufgabe*, the quasi-need, the *Bewusstseinslage*, interest and subjective value, prejudice, stereotype, and even the broadest conception of all, the philosophy of life. It excludes those types of readiness which are expressly innate, which are bound rigidly and invariably to the stimulus, which lack flexibility, and which lack directionality and reference to some external or conceptual object.

An attitude is a mental and neural state of readiness, organized through experience, exerting a directive or dynamic influence upon the individual's response to all objects and situations with which it is related. [. . .]

References

ALLPORT, F. H. (1924), *Social Psychology*, Houghton Mifflin.

ALLPORT, G. W. (1929), 'The composition of political attitudes', *Amer. J. Sociol.*, vol. 35, pp. 220–38.

BALDWIN, G. M. (1901–1905), *Dictionary of Philosophy and Psychology*, 3 vols., Macmillan Co.

BOGARDUS, E. S. (1931), *Fundamentals of Social Psychology*, Appleton-Century-Crofts, p. 62, 2nd edn.

CANTRIL, H. (1934), 'Attitudes in the making', *Understanding the Child*, ch. 4, pp. 13–15.

CHAVE, E. G. (1928), 'A new type scale for measuring attitudes', *Relig. Educ.*, vol. 23, pp. 364–9.

DROBA, D. D., (1933), 'The nature of attitude', *J. soc. Psychol.*, vol. 4, pp. 444–63.

EWER, B. C. (1929), *Social Psychology*, Macmillan Co.

KÖHLER, W. (1929), *Gestalt Psychology*, Liveright.

KRUEGER, E. T., and RECKLESS, W. C. (1931), *Social Psychology*, Longman.

LUNDBERG, G. A. (1929), *Social Research*, Longman.

MORGAN, J. J. B. (1934), *Keeping a Sound Mind*, Macmillan Co.

MURPHY, G., and MURPHY, L. B. (1931), *Experimental Social Psychology*, Harper & Row.

THOMAS, W. T., and ZNANIECKI, F. (1918), *The Polish Peasant in Europe and America*, vol. 1, Badger.

WARREN, H. C. (1922), *Elements of Human Psychology*, Houghton Mifflin.

WARREN, H. C. (1934), *Dictionary of Psychology*, Houghton Mifflin.

2 L. L. Thurstone

The Measurement of Social Attitudes

Excerpt from L. L. Thurstone, 'The measurement of social attitudes',
Journal of Abnormal and Social Psychology, vol. 26, 1931, pp. 249–69.

Our present definition of the term may be briefly stated as follows:
Attitude is the affect for or against a psychological object.

Affect in its primitive form is described as appetition or aversion.
Appetition is the positive form of affect which in more sophisticated
situations appears as liking the psychological object, defending it,
favoring it in various ways. Aversion is the negative form of affect
which is described as hating the psychological object, disliking it,
destroying it, or otherwise reacting against it. Attitude is here used
to describe *potential action* toward the object with regard only to
the question whether the potential action will be favorable or un-
favorable toward the object. For example, if we say that a man's
attitude toward prohibition is negative, we mean that his potential
actions about prohibition may be expected to be against it, barring
compromises in particular cases. When we say that a man's
attitude toward prohibition is negative, we have merely indicated
the affective direction of his potential action toward the object.
We have not said anything about the particular detailed manner
in which he might act. In this sense the term attitude is an ab-
straction in that it cannot be described without inserting the
cognitive details that are irrelevant; but this is also true of many of
the simplest concepts in daily use. [. . .]

3 C. A. Insko and J. Schopler

Triadic Consistency: A Statement of
Affective–Cognitive–Conative Consistency[1]

Excerpts from C. A. Insko and J. Schopler, 'Triadic consistency: a
statement of affective–cognitive–conative consistency',
Psychological Review, vol. 74, 1967, pp. 361–76.

Cohen (1964), Festinger (1964) and Greenwald (1965) have recently called attention to the neglect of research and theory
dealing with the relation between attitude change and behavior
change. There are numerous theories pertaining to the consistency
between attitudes (affect) and beliefs (cognitions), but, with the
possible exception of dissonance theory, there is no major theory
which attempts to extend consistency principles to relations between attitudes, beliefs, and behavior (conation).[2] This paper is an
attempt to develop such a theory based on the consistency between
the triad of affect, cognition and conation. Each of these concepts
will be discussed separately before turning to an analysis of the
manner in which they are interrelated.

Basic concepts
Attitudes and objects of affective significance

Attitudes are evaluative feelings of pro or con, favorable or un-
favorable, with regard to particular objects. Traditionally the
objects are considered to be either concrete representations of
things or actions (e.g. the Statue of Liberty, drinking), or abstract
concepts (e.g. democracy). When such objects have attitudes
directed toward them they are referred to as objects of affective
significance.

We would like to expand the meaning of abstract objects of
affective significance so that they may be propositions as well as
single concepts. This makes it possible, for example, to speak of

1. A preliminary draft of this paper was read by John Thibaut, James
Wiggins and Caryll Steffens. Their help is gratefully acknowledged.
2. After writing the initial draft of this paper in the spring of 1966, we
became aware of Fishbein's (1966) statement of the consistency between
attitudes, beliefs, and behavioral intentions.

attitudes held toward the proposition, 'it will rain
Any individual's attitude toward this proposition is an
value he places on the information contained in the pro
Attitude toward a proposition, however, is not the same t
belief in the truth of that proposition. Individuals may place quite
different values on a number of propositions, all of which are believed equally true. It is the case, however, that someone is not
likely to place much value on a disbelieved proposition and that the
greater the extent to which a proposition is believed the more likely
it is to be valued. There is thus an imperfect correlation between
belief in the truth of a given proposition and the value placed upon
that proposition.

Most consistency theorists, such as Heider (1958), Rosenberg
(1960), and Rosenberg and Abelson (1960) classify objects of
affective significance as either positive or negative. Osgood and
Tannenbaum (1955), on the other hand, scale the objects of
affective significance, or objects of judgement as they call them,
from extremely pro to extremely con in terms of semantic differ-
ential responses. For most purposes we will content ourselves with
a simple classification of objects of affective significance as either
positive or negative through the assigning of signs to these objects.
For some purposes, however, we will wish to refer to degrees of
polarization or the degrees to which an object is positively or
negatively evaluated.

Beliefs or cognitions

Cognitions are beliefs about or perceptions of relationship between
two objects of affective significance. For example, the perception
or belief that education contributes to a higher standard of living
is a cognition about the relationship between two objects of
affective significance, education and a higher standard of living.
Two additional examples of cognitions are: Bill is married to Jane,
and Bill likes Jane. In the first of these additional examples Bill is
perceived as having or is believed to have a marital relation to Jane.
In the second example Bill is perceived as having or is believed to
have a positive attitude toward Jane. Note that the last example is
a cognition about an attitude.

One of the primary problems facing consistency theories is that
of defining cognitions and specifying the difference between

tive and negative cognitions. Our approach is to define a cognition as *any perceived relationship*. While it is our intention to be completely inclusive, it is evident that some statements of relationships are cast in a form which does not readily permit the application of consistency principles. It is our assumption that such difficulties can be resolved by a careful examination of the meanings implied or by obtaining more information about the particular relationship at issue. In order to facilitate this goal we have tentatively characterized relations by a number of dimensions. This initial taxonomy is of affective, logical, instrumental, and spatially or temporally proximal dimensions.

Many cognitive relations seem to involve pure illustrations of these dimensions; other relations, however, seem to represent combinations of these dimensions or less obvious illustrations of single dimensions. 'Ownership' seems to involve a combination of affect, spatial proximity, and instrumentality. 'Is related to' implies some unspecified combination of all four types of relations. 'Is north of' is a spatial relation that would be considered positive if the distance is minimal and null if the distance is great. 'Is part of' is both a logical and a spatial relation. 'Similarity' is a type of logical relation because it involves an equivalence of common attributes or characteristics. 'Is characterized by' is a logical relation because it implies class inclusion. Other relations that are not stated in the present tense (e.g. 'has helped') involve null temporal proximity in addition to whatever else is implied. And finally, relations implying moral imperative or obligation (e.g. 'should help') imply an instrumental relation between carrying out certain activities and receiving certain goals.

The cognitive relations are further subdivided according to whether they are positive, negative or null. The null relations are negations of either positive or negative relations. They are always passive. Positive relations involve a perceptual tendency to work toward unity and negative relations involve a perceptual tendency to work toward disunity. For example, there is a perceptual tendency to group people together who like each other, help each other, stand next to each other, or are similar to each other. Likewise there is a tendency to perceive disunity between two people who hate each other, hinder each other, or are dissimilar to each other. Positive and negative relations are always active in the sense that they involve cognitive processes which work either toward or against perceived unity. At least to our phenomenology, spatial or temporal proximity may be positive or null, but not negative. Insofar as being separated implies nothing more than spatial separation this relation does not seem to imply a force toward disunity. One reason for undertaking a taxonomy of relationships is to be explicit about whether or not a given dimension has a negative pole, thereby avoiding attempts to apply the theory to inappropriate situations.

Just as objects of affective significance can be scaled on an evaluative dimension, it would be possible to scale cognitions on an intensity dimension. There is clearly a difference between saying 'A is fond of B' and 'A loves B'. Such differences may related to the compellingness with which consistency is achieved. [. . .]

Behavior or conation

In agreement with most contemporary psychologists we regard behavior as being goal-directed activity or striving. It consists of motor responses. Individuals typically evaluate their behavior as either plus or minus. To some extent the evaluation is dependent upon the pleasant or unpleasant hedonic sensations arising from the behavior, and to some extent the evaluation is dependent upon the behavior's instrumental or expressive worth. In general, we will not be concerned about the source or cause of the behavioral evaluation but simply assign the behavior a plus or minus depending upon the person's evaluative reaction to his own behavior. By and large such evaluations can be assumed to be positive.

Although the distinction between behavior and attitudes seems quite clear, a potential source of confusion exists because behaviors can also be objects of affective significance. For our purposes it is important to differentiate motoric behavior, for example the act of smoking, from the concept of some behavior, for example 'smoking'. Whenever we use the term 'behavior' we mean the actual occurrence of motor activity and not the simple concept of some motor activity.

Cognitive–affective consistency

Following Rosenberg and Abelson (1960) we will refer to affective-cognitive units as cognitive bands. Cognitive bands are simply two objects of positive or negative affective significance linked by a positive or negative cognition. Note that two objects of affective significance linked by a null cognition are not a cognitive band. In agreement with Cartwright and Harary's (1956) graph theory statement of Heider's (1958) balance theory position we propose that whenever the product of the signs is positive the cognitive band is consistent and whenever the product of the signs is negative the cognitive band is inconsistent. [. . .]

If a cognitive band is inconsistent there will be a *tendency* to resolve the inconsistency. Taking a cue from Osgood and Tannenbaum (1955) we further propose that *the greater the polarity in the linked objects of affective significance the greater will be the tendency to resolve inconsistency*. In disagreement with Osgood and Tannenbaum, however, we believe that attempted inconsistency reduction can take a number of forms other than a modification of the polarity or signs of the associated objects of judgement. For example, there may be a change in the sign of the linking cognitive relation, a differentiating or fragmenting of the objects of affective significance, or an attempt to 'drown out' the inconsistency through the bolstering of one or more of the objects of affective significance. Abelson (1959) has detailed a variety of such reactions to inconsistency.

Triadic consistency

It is the basic tenet of triadic consistency theory that there is a tendency for attitudes, cognitions and behaviors to be consistently related.

Cognitive–affective–conative consistency

Attitudes are linked to behavior via cognitive relations. We will refer to the affective–cognitive–conative linkage as a triad. Since each of the three elements of the triad can be assigned positive or negative signs it is possible to apply Cartwright and Harary's multiplication rule to determine whether or not consistency exists. If the product of all three signs is positive the triad is consistent; if the product of all three signs is negative the triad is inconsistent. For example, consider the attitude of a soldier toward his rifle. The cognitive relation between military role behavior and rifle is a positive instrumental and spatial one. Rifles are perceived as being close to and facilitating military behavior. Thus if the soldier evaluates his role behavior positively he should have a tendency to evaluate his rifle positively $(+ + + = +)$. On the other hand, if he evaluates his role behavior negatively he should have a tendency to evaluate his rifle negatively $(- + - = +)$.

While common sense seems to expect a high degree of cognitive–affective–conative consistency, research on this problem is ambiguous. [. . .] Most evidence with regard to affective–cognitive–conative consistency is, undoubtedly, considered so unexciting that researchers typically may make very little of it. Much such evidence probably is not even considered worthy of publication. What journal, for example, would accept an article showing that military officers have more positive attitudes toward various types of weapons than do matched non-military people?

Of course, attitudes, cognitions and behavior are not necessarily consistent, but we will assume there is a tendency toward such consistency. Stated in more operational terms, we are arguing that there is a probabilistic relation between holding certain beliefs and attitudes and manifesting certain behaviors.

We will now turn to the major purpose of the paper – a detailed examination of the movement toward triadic consistency, first, as affective–cognitive change following behavior change and, second, as behavior change following affective–cognitive change.

Affective–cognitive change as a consequence of behavior change

Typically, when someone engages in new behaviors he will be aware of the relationships between these new behaviors and various objects of affective significance. In some instances, however, new behaviors may be engaged in gradually so that the individual is aware of no new relations with any objects of affective significance. This is particularly likely if the objects are not very immediately related to the new behaviors. In any event, in order for the tendency toward consistency to operate following behavior change, the individual must be aware of new cognitive relationships. This tendency may operate so as to modify the sign of the attitude object. [. . .]

We would like to generalize that, *given triadic inconsistency, the greater the polarity of some new behavior and the associated object or objects of affective significance, the greater the tendency of the new behavior to produce a change toward consistency and away from inconsistency*. This change may be manifested through attitude change, a change in the perceived cognitive relation, or a differentiation of the object of affective significance. Because of the immediacy of many of the cognitive relations surrounding behavior we are inclined to think, however, that a change in the sign of a cognitive relation is not as likely as a change in the sign or polarity of the attitude. In general, we regard attitude change as the most likely mode of inconsistency resolution in any situation in which new behavior occurs.

Two additional considerations affecting the tendency of new behavior to produce a change toward consistency and away from inconsistency are the commitment the person holds with respect to the new behavior and the intensity or 'compellingness' of the cognition relating the behavior and object of affective significance. *The greater the commitment to the new behavior the greater the tendency toward consistency and away from inconsistency*. Although the concept of 'commitment' has several possible referents, we would define it in terms of a combination of the degree of irrevocability of the act and the importance of the act to the actor. In operational terms the distinction among private decision, public announcement and active participation in an activity related to an existing attitude represent increasing degrees of commitment. The intensity of a cognition has to do with how obvious and compelling the relation between the behavior and attitude may be. In general, *the greater the intensity of a cognitive relation the greater the likelihood of new behavior to produce a tendency toward consistency and away from inconsistency*. Counter-attitudinal advocacy is one way of producing a highly intense or compelling cognitive relation between behavior and attitude. [. . .]

Behavior change as a consequence of cognitive–affective change

The literature on the effect of cognitive–affective change upon behavior change is seemingly inconsistent. Some investigators have found that persuasive manipulations produce overt behavioral changes and some have found that they do not. [. . .]

In analysing the relation between cognitive–affective change and behavior change it is important to keep in mind that cognitive change can involve either a change in a cognitive band or a change in a triad. Cognitive change in a cognitive band involves a change in the perceived relationship between two objects of affective significance and cognitive change in a triad involves a change in the perceived relationship between an object of affective significance and behavior. The former change is illustrated by the communicatee who is persuaded that segregated Negro housing *inhibits the attainment* of an affective object, American prestige in other countries. The latter change is illustrated by the communicatee who is persuaded that his smoking behavior may contribute to an object of affective significance, lung cancer.

As Rosenberg (1960) has made evident, attitude change frequently occurs as a consequence of cognitive change in a cognitive band. For example, if the communicatee is convinced that segregation inhibits the attainment of American prestige in other countries his attitude toward segregation may change from positive to negative. In any event, once attitude change has occurred, does this mean that behavior change will also occur? A review of studies indicates that this is not necessarily so. There are a number of reasons for this. First, in order for any tendency toward triadic consistency to operate it is necessary that the individual perceive the relationship between his new attitude and some behavior. Consider, for example, the individual who is newly convinced that civil rights for Negroes is a good thing. Just because the individual has a new or different attitude toward civil rights doesn't mean that he will perceive 'what he can do'. Of course, the communication or series of communications that resulted in this new attitude may attempt to point out what sort of action should be taken, such as, for example, lying in the street with a group of protestors. There is no guarantee, however, that the individual will agree with this recommendation. In any event, before attitude change can result in behavior change the individual must perceive and accept the cognitive relation between the new attitude and some behavior.

A second reason why attitude change may not result in behavior change relates to various hedonistic considerations. People will be reluctant to enact negative behaviors; furthermore, people will be reluctant to enact behaviors that have negative instrumental relations to positive goals or positive instrumental relations to negative goals. The first of these considerations involves what may be called hedonism of the present and the second hedonism of the future. Hedonism of the present dictates that positive behaviors will occur and that negative behaviors will not. Hedonism of the future dictates that behaviors, of whatever sign, that facilitate positive goals or hinder negative goals will occur and behaviors, of whatever sign, that hinder positive goals or facilitate negative goals will not occur.[3] [. . .] This means that in some instances the tendency away from inconsistency may be overcome by one or the other of the two types of hedonism.

Rosenberg and Abelson (1960) have pointed out that a consistency or balance point of view can account for hedonistic tendencies in terms of hedonic bands involving the self. Since the self can typically be assumed to have positive evaluation, the self (+) in association with (+) a pleasant state of affairs (+) will be balanced and the self (+) in association with (+) an unpleasant state of affairs (−) will be imbalanced. Thus with the concept of hedonistic bands involving the self it is possible to translate the hedonic tendencies into simple tendencies toward consistency and away from inconsistency. Therefore even though the enactment of the behavior in a given triad would produce triadic consistency, the behavior may not occur if inconsistency in a hedonic band would be the result. [. . .]

A third reason why attitude change does not necessarily result in behavior change is simply that even if the relationship between the new attitude and positive behavior is perceived, opportunities for the behavior may not arise. Circumstances may prevent the individual from being confronted with a situation in which he has a choice between engaging in behavior that is either consistent or inconsistent with the new attitude. Why then, it may be asked, does not the individual seek out behavioral opportunities that will allow triadic consistency? It is true that there may be some tendency to seek out behavioral opportunities that will allow for triadic consistency. Such behavior, however, will be motivated by the tendency toward consistency and not by the tendency to reduce inconsistency. If an individual has a positive attitude toward an object of affective significance and perceives a positive cognitive relation toward certain behavior, we have two pluses and a

3. Rosenberg (1965) has investigated the effect of hedonism of the future in determining reactions to various cognitive bands.

nothing. There is no inconsistency and consequently no push to resolve inconsistency by engaging in certain behaviors. The fact, therefore, that the individual will be motivated to seek out behavioral opportunities by the tendency toward consistency, but not by the tendency to reduce inconsistency, is the main reason why the motivation is not particularly strong.

Situations in which the individual is faced with the choice of engaging in behavior that is perceived as being attitudinally relevant will be referred to as choice confrontations. If the individual has a choice confrontation, then there is a much greater likelihood of consistent behavior occurring. (Note that Greenwald's study (1965) in which attitude change was followed by a choice confrontation is one of the few studies finding evidence for an attitude change producing behavior change.) Choice confrontations are of three basic types: (a) confrontations which involve a choice as to whether or not to engage in consistent behavior, (b) confrontations which involve a choice as to whether or not to engage in inconsistent behavior, and (c) confrontations which involve a choice between engaging in consistent or inconsistent behavior. [...] This last type of situation is most likely to produce consistent behavior, first, because the individual has a clear choice between consistent and inconsistent behavior, and, second, because more than one triad is involved. The comparative rarity of these situations is an additional reason why behavior consistent with attitude change does not have a greater frequency of occurrence.

A final reason why consistent behavior may not occur relates to the existence of competing triads. *Positive behavior that balances a given triad will tend not to occur if that behavior simultaneously imbalances a second triad involving a more polarized object of affective significance.* Consider the example of the person who, after adopting a favorable attitude toward civil rights, is solicited to contribute money to a given civil rights organization. If the individual perceives that contributing money would facilitate the attainment of civil rights there will be a tendency to make a contribution and balance the triad. However, suppose that contributing money to civil rights would prevent the individual from having enough money to pay his rent on time. If the individual perceives that contributing money (+) would prevent (−) paying the rent on time (+) there will be a tendency not to engage in the inconsistent contributing behavior. How will the individual resolve the conflict? Assuming that he has only the choice of contributing or not contributing the conflict may be resolved in terms of the relative polarities of the objects of affective significance. Which object of affective significance does the individual value most highly, civil rights or paying the rent on time? If the individual places a higher value on paying the rent on time than on civil rights, then there will be a tendency not to contribute his limited funds to civil rights. An additional consideration influencing his behavior is the relative polarity of the two behaviors, contributing and not contributing. If contributing is more pleasant than not contributing, then there will be a greater hedonic push toward contributing.

The above situation, however, may be even more complicated. The individual may realize that he could contribute to civil rights and then work nights so as to earn additional money for the rent. This however may create inconsistency if he perceives that working nights (+) would prevent (−) him from associating with his family (+). *Assuming equal polarities of the attitudes involved the individual will tend to act so as to balance the maximum number of triads.* If the polarities are not equal more weight will be given to the triads with the polarized attitudes. These considerations make it obvious that the causal link between the acquisition of a new attitude (for example, a positive attitude toward civil rights) and the enactment of seemingly consistent behavior (for example, contributing to a civil rights organization) is not a very direct one. What seems consistent in terms of a closed system involving one triad may not be maximally consistent when attention is paid to the total matrix of triads.

In the above section we have detailed a number of factors that effect the causal link between attitude change and behavior change. These factors include whether or not the relationship between the new attitude and consistent behavior is perceived, various hedonistic considerations, the existence of opportunities for consistent behavior, the motivational strength to seek out opportunities for consistent behavior, the nature of choice confrontations, and the existence of competing triads. A consideration of all of these factors makes the inconsistency of the literature on this topic more understandable. Without further information regarding these various factors it simply cannot be predicted that attitude change will necessarily lead to behavior change.

We are inclined to believe that the causal link from behavior change to attitude change is both stronger and more direct than is the causal link from attitude change to behavior change. The basis for this belief is that some of the above factors do not apply or less obviously apply to the behavior–change–attitude–change sequence. Hedonism of the present is not a factor preventing attitude change and the individual does not have to wait for an appropriate environmental situation for attitude change or actively seek out such a situation. It is true, though, that competing cognitive bands may decrease the probability of attitude change. We are, however, in general inclined to believe that most of the triadic consistency existing in the social environment results from attitudes being adapted so as to be consistent with behavior.

References

ABELSON, R. P. (1959), 'Modes of resolution of belief dilemmas', *J. Conflict Resolution*, vol. 3, pp. 343–52.

CARTWRIGHT, D., and HARARY, F. (1956), 'Structural balance: a generalization of Heider's theory', *Psychol. Rev.*, vol. 63, pp. 277–93.

COHEN, A. R. (1964), *Attitude Change and Social Influence*, Basic Books.

FESTINGER, L. (1964), 'Behavioral support for opinion change', *Pub. Opinion Q.*, vol. 28, pp. 404–17.

FISHBEIN, M. (1966), 'The relationship between beliefs, attitudes, and behavior', in S. Feldman (ed.), *Cognitive Consistency: Motivational Antecedents and Behavioral Consequents*, Academic Press, pp. 199–233.

GREENWALD, A. G. (1965), 'Behavior change following a persuasive communication', *J. Pers.*, vol. 33, pp. 370–91.

HEIDER, F. (1958), *The Psychology of Interpersonal Relations*, Wiley.

OSGOOD, C. E., and TANNENBAUM, P. H. (1955), 'The principle of congruity in the prediction of attitude change', *Psychol. Rev.*, vol. 62, pp. 42–55.

ROSENBERG, M. J. (1960), 'An analysis of affective–cognitive consistency', in C. I. Hovland and M. J. Rosenberg (eds.), *Attitude Organization and Change*, Yale University Press, pp. 15–64.

ROSENBERG, M. J. (1965), 'Some determinants of intolerance for attitudinal inconsistency' in S. S. Tomkins and C. E. Izard (eds.), *Affect, Cognition and Personality*, Springer, pp. 130–47.

ROSENBERG, M. J., and ABELSON, R. P. (1960), 'An analysis of cognitive balancing', in C. I. Hovland and M. J. Rosenberg (eds.), *Attitude Organization and Change*, Yale University Press, pp. 112–63.

4 L. W. Doob

The Behaviour of Attitudes

Excerpt from L. W. Doob, 'The behavior of attitudes', *Psychological Review*, vol. 54, 1947, pp. 135-56.

There is no question that the subject of attitude and attitude measurements is important in sociology and social psychology. Social scientists continue to discuss the nature of attitudes in articles like this, to conduct experiments which show that behavior is affected by attitude, and to measure attitudes for theoretical or practical purposes. The problem of what an attitude is and how it functions, nevertheless, persists and – as many writers on attitudes likewise point out in their introductory paragraph – little explicit agreement is apparent in the published literature.

The purpose of this paper is not to criticize other definitions or usages of the term but systematically, if partially, to relate the concept of attitude to what is known as behavior theory (Hull, 1943).[1] Almost all writers, no matter what their bias, agree that attitudes are learned. If this is so, then the learning, retention, and decline of an attitude are no different from the learning of a skill, a piece of prose, or a set of nonsense syllables; and they must also involve the problems of perception and motivation.

Immediately it is necessary to raise and answer the question as to why a simple, commonsense, ubiquitous concept like attitude should be translated into semi-technical jargon. There are at least two answers to the question. The first and less important answer involves scientific methodology: it is thought desirable to bring as many terms as possible relating to a field of research (in this instance, human behavior) within one universe of discourse. Mis-

1. The writer is deeply grateful especially to Neal E. Miller as well as to Irvin L. Child, John Dollard and Mark A. May for their constructive criticisms. He has promiscuously and deliberately borrowed some of their ideas and, as an insignificant token of his gratitude, herewith absolves them of any responsibility for the final product.

understandings result from using one set of concepts to describe perception, learning and motivation on one level and another set on a different level. Even if some sociologists who use the concept 'attitude' are not attracted by the terminology of behavior theory and if they remain inclined merely to assume perception, learning and motivation without inquiring into the details of the processes, unified knowledge concerning human behavior requires that there be a connection between what the sociologist studies or measures and what the psychologist studies or measures. Secondly, and of crucial importance, a tentative translation of a term from one level to another and into an already and perhaps better developed theoretical system is fully justified if thereby inadequacies on the higher level can be pointed out. Murray and Morgan (1945), for example, have recently shed new light on the nature of attitude by incorporating the closely related concept of sentiment into the former's previous conceptualization of personality.

The procedure to be followed in this paper is as follows:

1. A definition of attitude in behavioral terms will be given. It is felt that such a definition represents an advance beyond the stage of defining an attitude as the subjective counterpart of something in the environment, as a predisposition within the organism, or as being what the attitude scale measures. The psychological implications of the definition will be made clear.

2. The consequences of this definition and the theoretical structure it assumes will then be summarized briefly by calling attention to the factors which should be known to make a completely adequate analysis of attitudes.

3. Illustrative research employing the concept of attitude will be critically examined in terms of these factors. Such a detailed examination seems preferable to surveying the attitude literature in general terms.

Definition of attitude

Attitude is defined as: *An implicit, drive-producing response considered socially significant in the individual's society.*

This definition states, in effect, that from the psychological point of view attitude is an implicit response with drive strength which occurs within the individual as a reaction to stimulus patterns and which affects subsequent overt responses. Since psychologists and other social scientists sometimes disagree concerning the nature and attributes of an implicit response of this type, the definition is therefore elaborated and broken down typographically into the phrases and clauses requiring further definition, elaboration and discussion:

An attitude is:

1. an implicit response,

2. which is both (*a*) anticipatory and (*b*) mediating in reference to patterns of overt responses,

3. which is evoked (*a*) by a variety of stimulus patterns (*b*) as a result of previous learning or of gradients of generalization and discrimination,

4. which is itself cue and drive-producing,

5. and which is considered socially significant in the individual's society.

1. *An attitude is an implicit response*. . . . By an implicit response is meant a response occurring within the individual and not immediately observable to an outsider. Motor 'attitudes' like the physical set of the runner before the starter's gun is fired, therefore, are not included within the universe of discourse being analysed because they are not entirely implicit and hence are instrumental rather than mediating acts. The semantic connection of such sets with the concept of attitude employed by social scientists is considered to be largely fortuitous from an historical standpoint.

Overt behavior that is observable to an outsider may be affected by the evoked attitude but is not here defined as the attitude itself. Attitude refers to the individual's immediate but implicit response to a stimulus pattern and his consequent tendency to respond still further as a result of that implicit response. Such an implicit response may be conscious or unconscious, distinctly verbal or vaguely proprioceptive. What is expressed results not from the attitude alone but represents, as will be indicated, another response in a behavior sequence – an overt one – which is a function of the attitude-response and other tendencies within the individual.

2. (a) *An attitude is an implicit response which is . . . anticipatory . . . in reference to patterns of overt responses.* . . . An anticipatory response – called also an antedating response by Hull (1943, p. 74) – is one which originally preceded another rewarded response and which, as a result of being associated with or producing this reward, has been reinforced so that it occurs before its 'original time in the response series' (Miller and Dollard, 1941, p. 49). If an individual, for example, dislikes a fruit or a person, he tends to avoid eating the fruit or meeting the person. Originally the avoidance occurred only after actual contact had been established and after that contact had proven to be punishing and the withdrawal to be rewarding. When a thorough investigation reveals no actual prior contact, some process of generalization or discrimination must have occurred since all behavior has antecedents. The possibility of exceptions under different psychological conditions must be noted, even in these trivial illustrations: the fruit may be eaten anyhow if the individual is very hungry and the person may be met and greeted if social circumstances so require.

The conditions under which a response moves up in the behavior sequence and becomes anticipatory have so far been determined concretely in relatively simple situations. It has been shown (Miller and Dollard, 1941, p. 79), for example, that the closer the response is in the series leading to the reward, the more likely it is to be learned and then subsequently to antedate other responses not leading to the reward. This principle suggests why few objects or individuals in society fail to arouse attitudes. Originally the individual has had to react to them or has been taught to react to them in the course of being socialized. One of the responses leading to the goal response (which by definition involves reward or the avoidance of punishment) has implicit components, is reinforced, and is here called an attitude.

2. (b) *An attitude is an implicit response which is . . . mediating in reference to patterns of overt responses.* . . . Whereas the anticipatory character of attitude indicates its temporal relation to a goal, its mediating attribute calls attention to its functional connection with that goal. A mediating response is made in an attempt to increase the likelihood of the occurrence of reward rather than punishment in connection with a goal response. In reasoning, for

example, implicit responses intervene between the original stimulus pattern and the goal response and may assist the individual in achieving that goal. Attitudes can be evoked so easily because as mediating responses involving only language, imagery, or proprioceptive reactions they need not conflict with the overt behavior of the individual or with his environment.

The mediating function of attitude has led May to suggest that attitude is 'a kind of substitute goal response' which 'arises when the goal response cannot be immediately and easily made' (May, unpublished paper). This attribute, which has also been suggested by other writers (e.g. Bernard, 1926, pp. 425–6 and Richards, 1926, pp. 28–9), does seem to characterize certain attitudes. The individual who dislikes another person is restrained or restrains himself from hurting his antagonist; instead he makes an implicit response involving aggression and feelings of avoidance or repulsion. It is felt, however, that all attitudes cannot be so characterized. The liked object, for example, evokes an implicit response which facilitates rather than acts as a substitute for overt behavior in reference to it. Overt behavior, in short, may be mediated by attitudes almost immediately and there need not necessarily be a conflict or a restraint before the attitude is evoked.

Three consequences arise immediately from this conceptualization of attitude. In the first place, it appears psychologically futile – as Sherif and Cantril have indicated (1945, pp. 304–5) – to attempt to classify attitudes. Responses can be characterized in so many different ways that a simple dichotomy or trichotomy usually must be willfully stretched if it is to include all types of behavior. The response defined as attitude might be called positive or negative or be said to involve approach or withdrawal were it not for the fact that these terms then require further definition which cannot be consistently or usefully applied to all situations. Both approach and avoidance, for example, may be but are not necessarily involved in what has been called a neutral attitude or in any attitude for that matter. It seems better, in short, to apply *socially* useful labels to attitude as the need arises, in order to indicate the direction in which the individual thereby is oriented; but it should be clearly recognized that the labels have social and not psychological significance. A psychologically important distinction, however, is that between general and specific attitudes

(Cantril, 1932), a distinction which refers to the stimulus patterns evoking the response or to the evoked responses.

In the second place, reference is made in the definition to 'patterns of overt responses'. For reasons hereafter suggested, overt behavior can seldom be predicted from knowledge of attitude alone. Under varying conditions within the individual, a given attitude can mediate a repertoire of overt responses. A favorable attitude toward a social institution, for example, can mediate innumerable responses connected with what is considered to be the welfare of that institution.

Then, thirdly, this definition of attitude emphasizes its acquired or learned character. There are no psychic rays which enable the investigator, even though he be equipped with a poll or a scale, to determine the 'strength' of an attitude, the overt responses with which it has become associated, or its present functioning within the personality. Such knowledge can be obtained only from knowing approximately under what conditions the attitude was acquired in the first place and the extent to which it secures present and future reinforcement. The learning process, therefore, is crucial to an understanding of the behavior of attitudes.

The nature of that process cannot be ignored in a treatise on attitude as it has been by Sherif and Cantril: 'Just what the psychological or physiological mechanisms of this learning may be are irrelevant to the present discussion', they write in their articles on 'The psychology of "attitudes"' (1945, p. 302). It is difficult to see how psychologists can call these mechanisms 'irrelevant' and still contend, as the authors do in the introduction to the same articles, that the 'task' of the psychologist is to 'give an adequate account of the psychological mechanisms involved in the formation of an attitude in any individual' (1945, p. 295). The authors rest their case by stating that they 'do not need to take sides in favor of any learning theory' (1945, p. 307). Of course, as they write, 'the primary stage in the formation of attitudes is a perceptual stage', which is merely saying that there must be a stimulus and that the stimulus must be perceived before there can be any kind of learning.

In contrast, Allport (1935, pp. 810–12) has set the problem of the genesis of attitudes in terms which explicitly suggest the need for learning theory. His often quoted summary of the literature indicates that attitudes may be formed through 'the integration of numerous specific responses of a similar type'; 'individuation, differentiation, or segregation' of experiences; 'trauma'; and the adoption of 'ready-made' attitudes of others. The genesis of almost any attitude is undoubtedly more or less unique. Society sets the rewards and punishments regarding much of overt behavior; the individual being socialized then is forced into the learning situation; although he reacts to the situation uniquely, one of the end products – the attitude – he may share in large degree with others.

3. (a) *An attitude is an implicit response . . . which is evoked by a variety of stimulus patterns. . . .* The stimuli evoking an attitude may be in the external world or within the individual. The latter range from a verbal response to an autonomic disturbance or a drive. The existing literature on attitudes testifies to the fact that the stimuli may be various. Such is the assumption behind any attitude scale in which a variety of situations is judged or behind a distinction like that between specific and general attitudes.

The arousal of an attitude involves two traditional problems in psychology, those of perception and learning. The two are interrelated and can be separated only for purposes of analysis. Perception indicates that the individual is responding because he has previously paid attention to or been oriented toward certain stimuli which then affect his sense organs and thus evoke his attitude. Learning in this connection emphasizes the reasons in the past history of the individual which have brought about the bond between the stimulus pattern and the attitude.

Gestalt psychologists especially point out that paying attention and then perceiving occur in many instances as a result of the individual's set to respond: letter boxes are not noticed unless the person has a letter to post, etc. Writers on attitude are fond of recalling that the tradition of set is somewhat hoary in academic psychology, in order to demonstrate their own respectability and their acquaintance with long German terms like *Bewusstseinslage*. In other words, perceiving depends upon drive or set (which orients the individual to respond to certain stimuli and then to respond to them in a particular way) as well as upon the arrangements of the external stimuli. Attitude may be included among the sets determining both the orientation of the individual as well as the kind of perceptual response he makes: the southerner notices incipient aggression in a Negro which a northerner will overlook.

It must be recognized, however, that in some situations the individual's attitude is not evoked until the stimulus has been actually perceived: it affects perception after its arousal but does not orient him originally in the direction of the stimuli involved. The southerner who has learned to discriminate incipient hostility from genuine docility among Negroes can make the discrimination when confronted with a Negro. It is on the basis of this discrimination that his attitude toward the Negro is or is not aroused. If he goes about the streets looking for hostility in Negroes, he may be set to make the discrimination not necessarily by his attitude toward Negroes or by his ability to detect such behavior but by some particular drive which has been previously aroused and which may or may not involve Negroes. To say that he searches for aggression solely because of his attitude toward Negroes is to fail to distinguish him from another southerner who has a more or less identical attitude (so far as content and even 'affect' are concerned) but who has no 'chip on his shoulder'. In this case the sensible problem remains of accounting for the 'chip'.

In controlled experimental situations dedicated to observing the behavior of attitudes, the attention of the subjects is secured by the experimenter not through arousing the attitude being studied but through the evocation of some other drive. Subjects perceived the autokinetic phenomenon of Sherif (1935) or they looked at Seeleman's photographs of white and colored individuals (1940) because they had agreed to cooperate with the experimenter. This was the drive which oriented them in the experimental situation. Then their attitudes were aroused and these attitudes affected both their perceptual responses and the reports they gave the experimenters. Later on in the experiments, their evoked attitudes may have had sufficient drive strength also to orient them selectively.

3. (b) *An attitude is an implicit response . . . which is evoked . . . as a result of previous learning or of gradients of generalization and discrimination. . . .* The previous section has indicated the possible relation between perception and the evocation of an attitude and

therein it was suggested that an attitude can almost always be aroused by a variety of stimuli. Here it is stated that previous learning determines whether or not particular stimulus patterns will evoke the attitude. Some stimuli come to arouse an attitude after a relatively simple process of conditioning has occurred. As a result of being originally present in the situation, for example, the wrapper of the disliked fruit or the signature of the disliked person may produce an anticipatory response which mediates the goal response of avoiding it or him. Other stimuli evoke or fail to evoke an attitude not because of their presence or absence in previous situations but because they fall along a stimulus gradient of generalization or discrimination. If an individual likes or dislikes one particular Negro, there is stimulus discrimination; if all Negroes are involved, there is stimulus generalization along a gradient, for example, of skin color; if only certain 'types' of Negroes arouse the attitude, there is generalization and discrimination.

Frequently attitudes are thought to be puzzling and mysterious because they can be aroused when the psychologist, the sociologist, the layman and the individual least expect them to be. The stimulus pattern, for example, may be a word or a sentence, or some other symbol (like a flag, a face or a gesture) which represents only a portion of the original stimulus pattern. The behavior of attitudes under these circumstances, however, becomes more intelligible when the implications of the 'gradient of generalization and discrimination' are understood. This gradient is specially efficacious in the case of attitude since language can readily perform the function of mediating generalization and discrimination. Cofer and Foley (1942), for example, are able a priori to list over fifty gradients along which generalization or discrimination from a single word can conceivably occur in purely formal (i.e. in non-idiosyncratic) manner. The word 'Negro', for example, through previous learning may become the one part of the original stimulus pattern which evokes an attitude regarding Negroes. Without any difficulty there can be a semantic gradient including words like 'colored', 'African', and the various epithets and appellations applied to this group. Through a slightly more complicated process, eventually 'zoot suit' may arouse the same attitude: if the individual has associated this type of clothing with

Negroes, the response of seeing such clothing or hearing its name evokes the internal response of 'Negro' which in turn has the property of arousing the attitude. This phenomenon has been called secondary stimulus generalization or acquired cue value. Similarly, thinking can aid generalization and discrimination.

Cantril in his work on attitudes fails to comprehend this stimulus gradient involved in most if not all learning and conditioning. He states, for example, that what he calls 'a standard of judgement' must not be 'confused with a conditioned response' (1941, p. 25). What he means by 'a standard of judgement' or a 'frame of reference' he never makes operationally clear, although they seem to be related to attitude since they are employed profusely in his two articles on the subject. It may be that terms like these – to use Cantril's own words in reference to 'conditioning' – are 'so loosely employed' that they 'explain nothing at all' (1941, p. 55). His conception of a conditioned response is indeed narrow: 'a specific reaction to a specific stimulus' (1941, p. 25). In spite of a general, noncommittal reference in a footnote to a standard book on conditioning (that of Hilgard and Marquis) and an irrelevant quotation from A. N. Whitehead, this simplification of behavior theory leads him to conclude that such a theory is by no means adequate to explain the apparent meaningfulness of man's experience' (1941, p. 56). More specifically, for example, he maintains that the 'analysis of the backgrounds of the people who became panicky listening to the Hallowe'en broadcast [of Orson Welles in 1938] clearly shows that in no way had they been specifically conditioned against Martian invaders' mowing down people on this planet' (1941, p. 25). The point of Cantril's study (Cantril, Gaudet and Herzog, 1940), however, is to discover the previously existing attitudes and traits which made people prone to panic or sanity. After discovering many of them with admirable ingenuity, he gives a commonsense 'explanation' of the behavior; i.e. he uses his particular vocabulary to describe what happened (1940, pp. 190–201). His failure to apply chapter 8 of Hilgard and Marquis (1940) to his own data prevents him from realizing that at the time of the broadcast people had learned to respond with anxiety to various stimuli as a result, for example, of the 'war scare' associated with the Munich crisis (cf. Cantril, Gaudet and Herzog, 1940, pp. 159–60). Certain Americans, some of whose socio-economic and psychological characteristics Cantril has indicated, apparently generalized from these stimuli to a broadcast which of course they had not previously experienced but which nevertheless was sufficiently similar to other stimulus patterns previously evoking the anxiety. Such individuals 'jumped the gun' by behaving – after their attitudes had been aroused by Mr Welles and his associates – as they would have in the face of genuine catastrophe.

From experiments in other fields of behavior, Hull states that the amplitude of a response 'diminishes steadily with the increase in the extent of deviation ... of the evocation stimulus ... from the stimulus originally conditioned ...' (1943, p. 185) and that 'the strength of the connections at other points of the zone can be determined only from a knowledge of the strength of the receptor-effector connection ... at the point of reinforcement and the extent of the difference ... between the position of the conditioned stimulus ... and that of the evocation stimulus ... on the stimulus continuum connecting them' (1943, p. 187). Whether or not the principle holds true of attitudes has not been tested, so far as this writer knows. To test it, it would be necessary to know 'the stimulus originally conditioned', the gradient along which the various 'evocation stimuli' are located, and whether or not in fact these latter stimuli have never been previously reinforced or extinguished. This could be done only by means of a careful life history of various individuals and by some objective measurement of the strength of the attitude.

At any rate, this generalization of Hull has an important bearing on the strength of attitude. The 'strength' of an attitude is almost as ambiguous as the concept of attitude itself. One type of strength that seems important for predicting future behavior of the individual is the *afferent-habit strength* of the attitude, i.e. the strength of the bond between the stimulus pattern and the response which is here defined as attitude. In these terms the afferent-habit strength of an attitude is a function of the number of previous reinforcements as well as the position along the gradient occupied by a particular stimulus pattern.

4. *An attitude is an implicit response ... which is itself cue and drive-producing.* ... Like all implicit responses, attitudes can be